THREE SHEETS
IN THE WIND

By Norman Thelwell

Three Sheets in the Wind
Up the Garden Path
Compleat Tangler
Play it as it Lies

·thelwell·

THREE SHEETS IN THE WIND

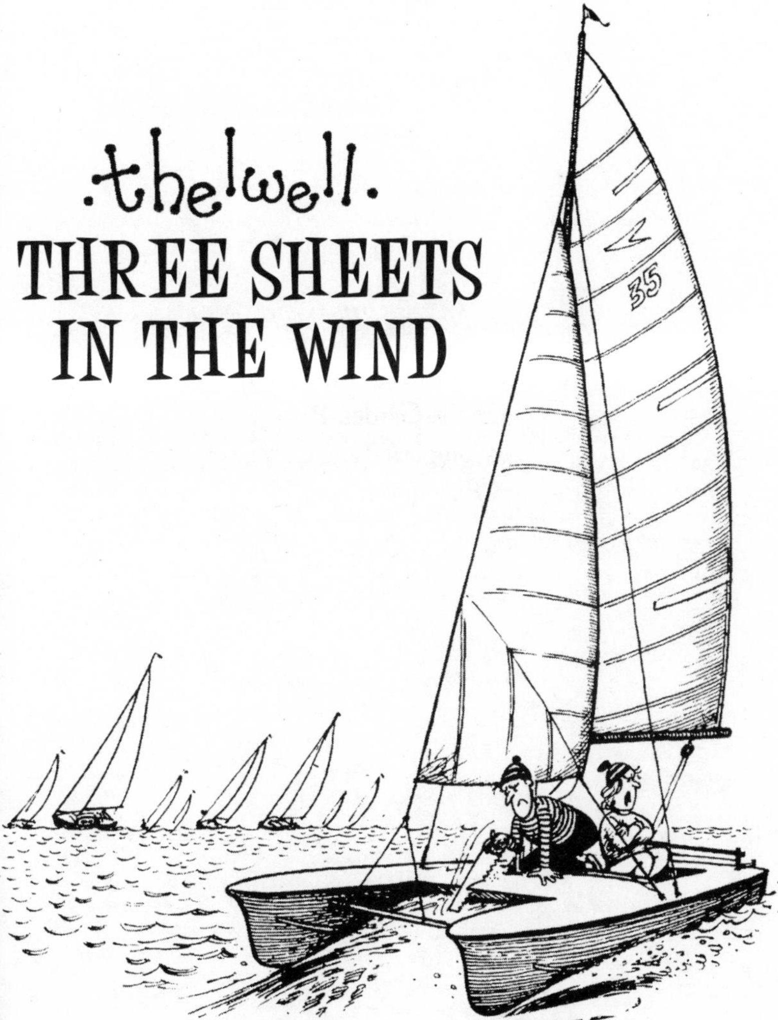
35

Allison & Busby Limited
12 Fitzroy Mews
London W1T 6DW
www.allisonandbusby.com

First published in 1973.
This edition published in Great Britain by Allison & Busby in 2014.

A CIP catalogue record for this book is available from
the British Library.

10 9 8 7 6 5 4 3 2 1

ISBN 978-0-7490-1716-3

Typeset in 10/15 pt Adobe Caslon Pro by
Allison & Busby Ltd.

The paper used for this Allison & Busby publication
has been produced from trees that have been legally sourced
from well-managed and credibly certified forests.

Printed and bound by
CPI Group (UK) Ltd, Croydon, CR0 4YY

CONTENTS

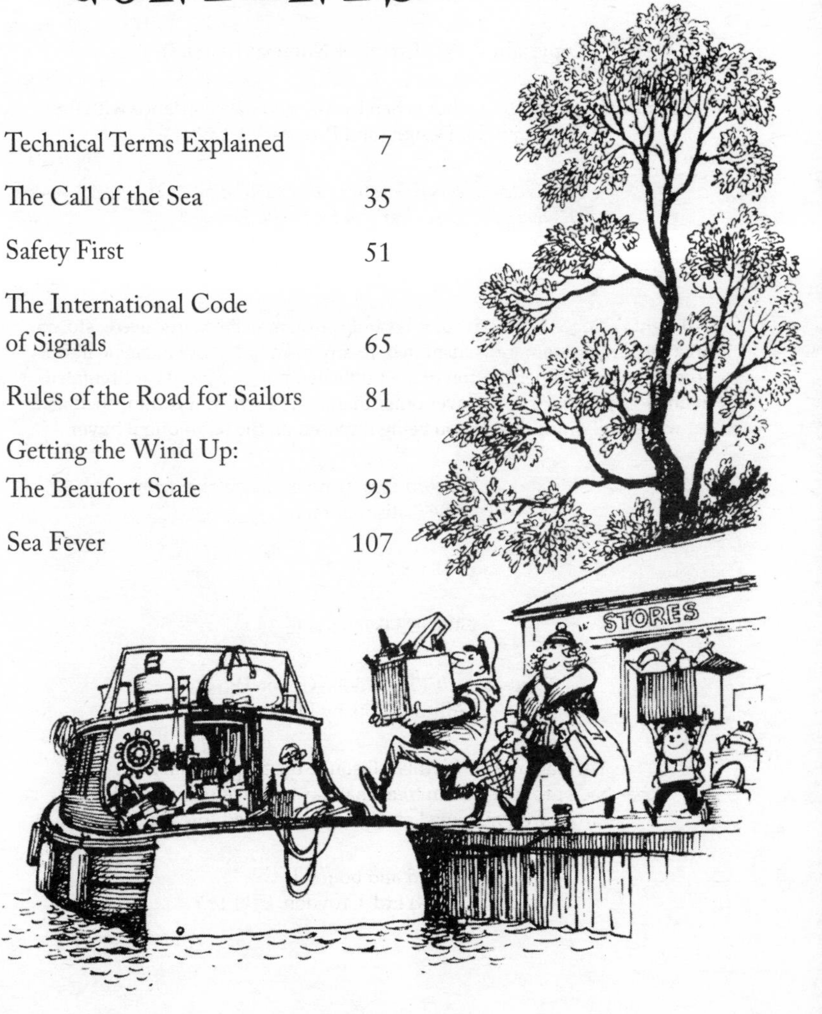

STORES

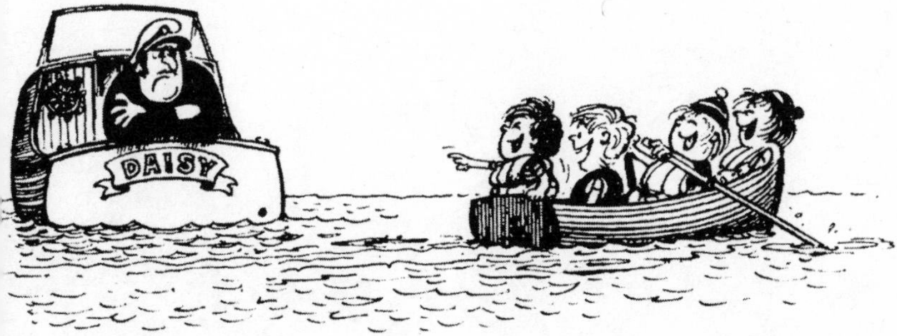
DAISY

TECHNICAL TERMS
EXPLAINED

DEAD WOOD
FORE PEAK
WEATHER EYE
BAGGY WRINKLE
EYE OF THE WIND
DIPPING LUG
POINT OF SAILING
TEETH OF THE GALE
JIB
GOOSE NECK
CROW'S NEST
SEAMAN'S CHEST
YARD ARM
(FOR A BROAD REACH)
PORT
OR DRAUGHT
CUTTER
(FOR TRIMMING SAIL)
SAG
UNDER WAY
SAILING CLUB
(FOR BEATING)
SEA LEGS
(FOR RUNNING BEFORE
THE WIND)
GROUND TACKLE
(FOR STEPPING THE MAST)
KICKING STRAP

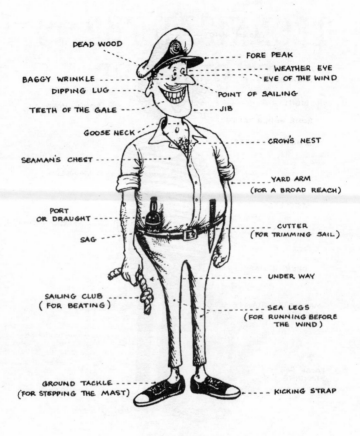

Guy Rope (Captain)

CROWN KNOT
LOOK OUTS
ROW LOCKS
BIGHT
BOOM JAWS
BONE IN HER TEETH
SAFETY HARNESS
FENDERS
MIDDLE GROUND
APPARENT WIND
DECK HANDS
MARINE INSURANCE (FOR LETTING FLY)
COMPASS (FOR LOSING WAY)
SHEEP SHANKS (FOR GOING ABOUT)
LOOSE FOOTED STANDING LUGS (FOR TRIPPING THE ANCHOR)
FOOT PUMPS
HEEL

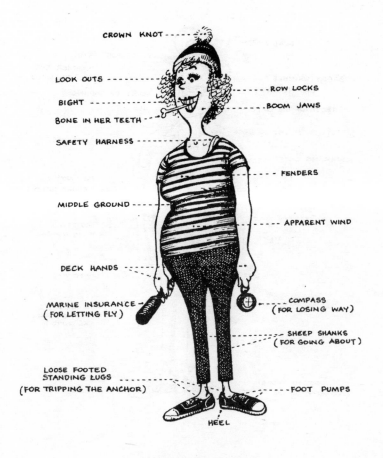

May Day (First Mate)

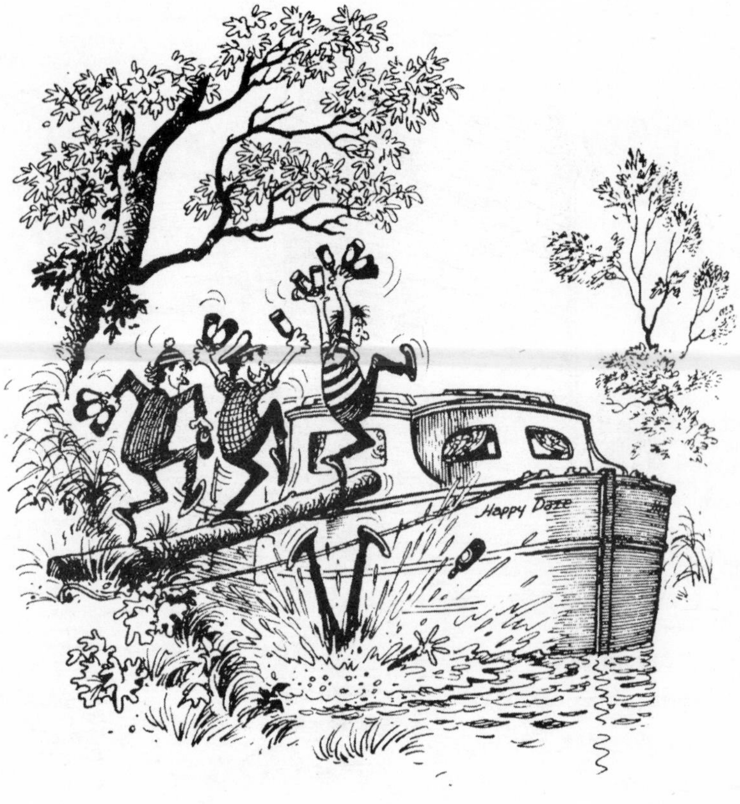
Happy Daze

Entering up the log

A sailor's bunk

A sea shanty

Free board

Capsize

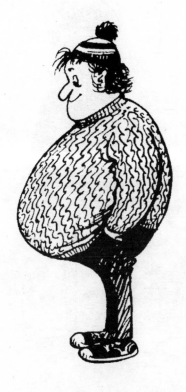

Personal buoyancy

Reef points

Flinder's bar

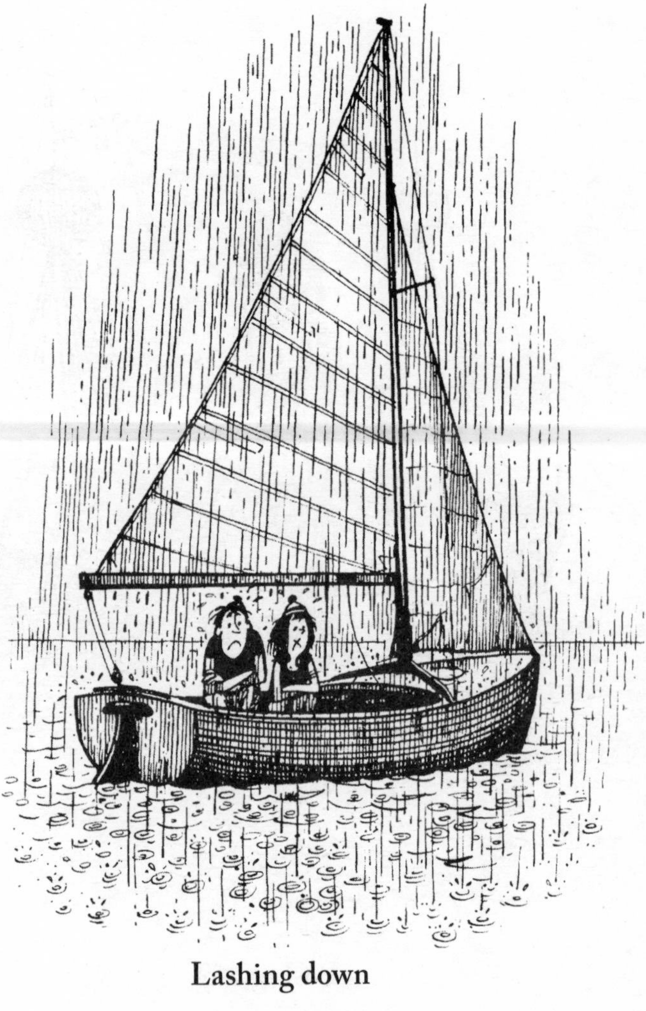

Lashing down

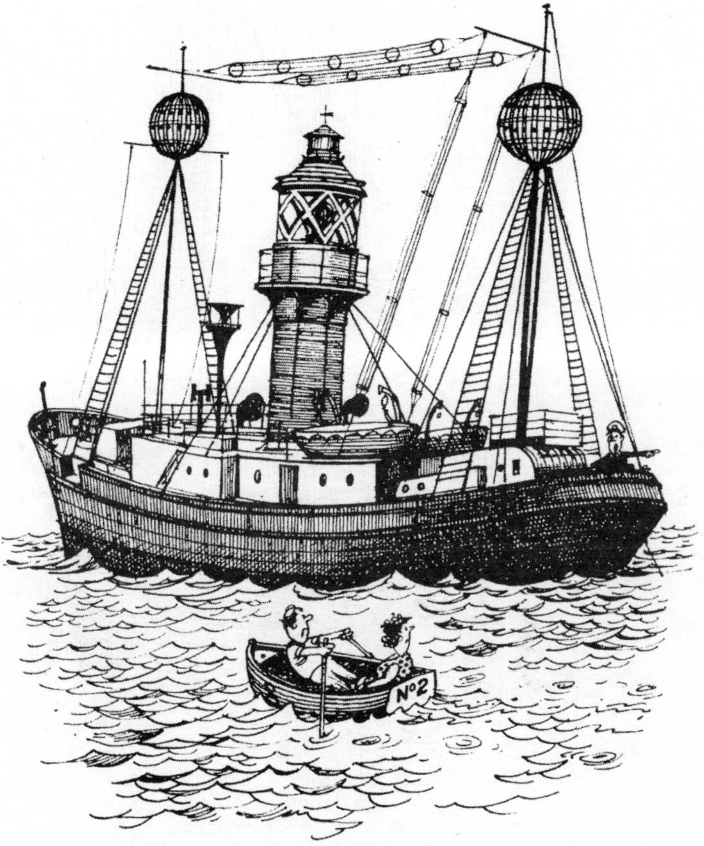
No2

Losing way

Boom

22

A windlass

Dressed overall

Making sail

A sailing horse

Tide race

Navigation marks

By and large

Lying in the roads

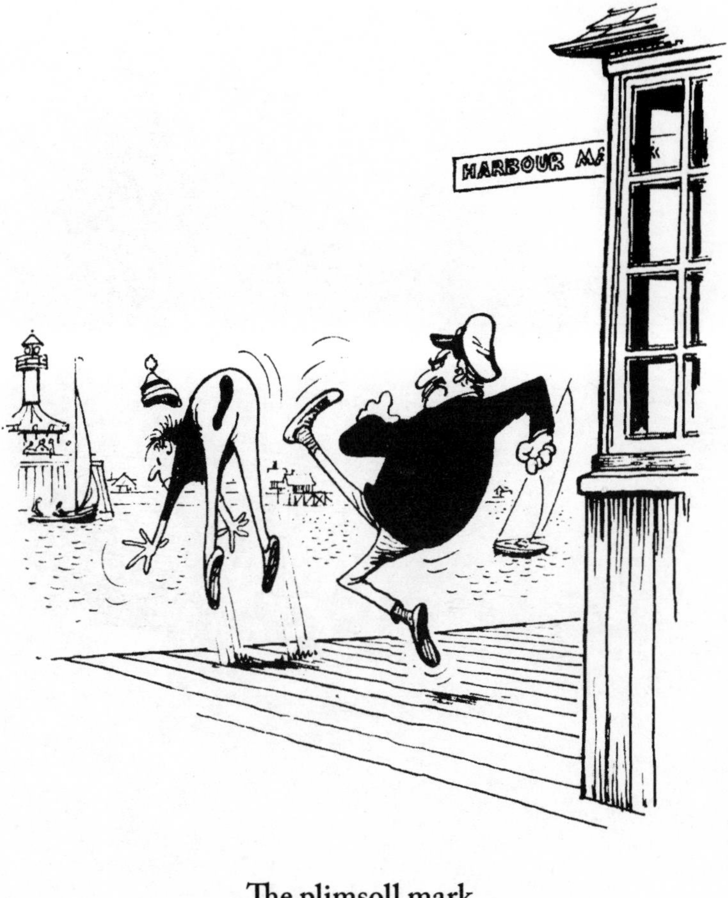
HARBOUR MA

The plimsoll mark

'Where's this place, mate?'

THE CALL
OF THE SEA

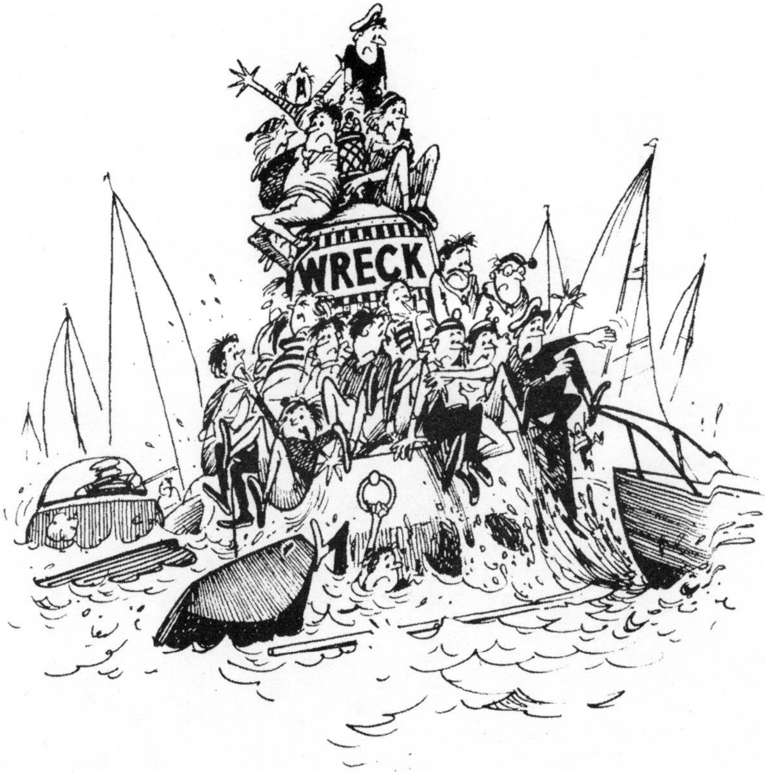
WRECK

Sailing is the fastest growing participation sport of modern times.

It is no longer the exclusive preserve of the very rich.

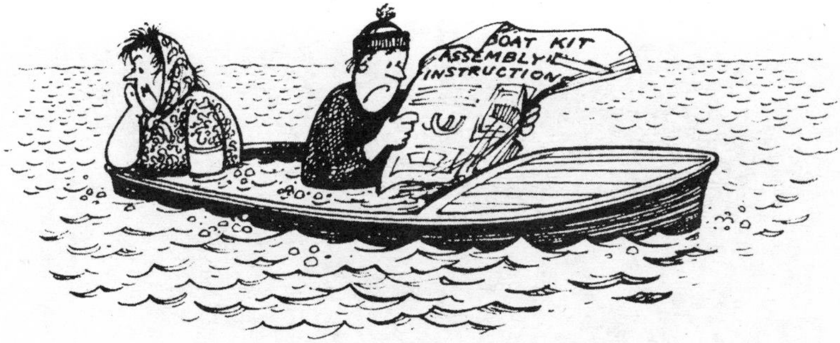
BOAT KIT
ASSEMBLY
INSTRUCTIONS

Nor does one have to be wealthy to own one's own craft.

Sailing is a family sport.

There is no room for the generation gap in a boat.

Whether your preference is for the feel of a
capricious breeze in your canvas

or for the heady excitement of a surging power boat . . .

whether you find yourself drawn irresistibly to
the open sea

or take your pleasures in inland waters –
there is nothing quite like the thrill . . .

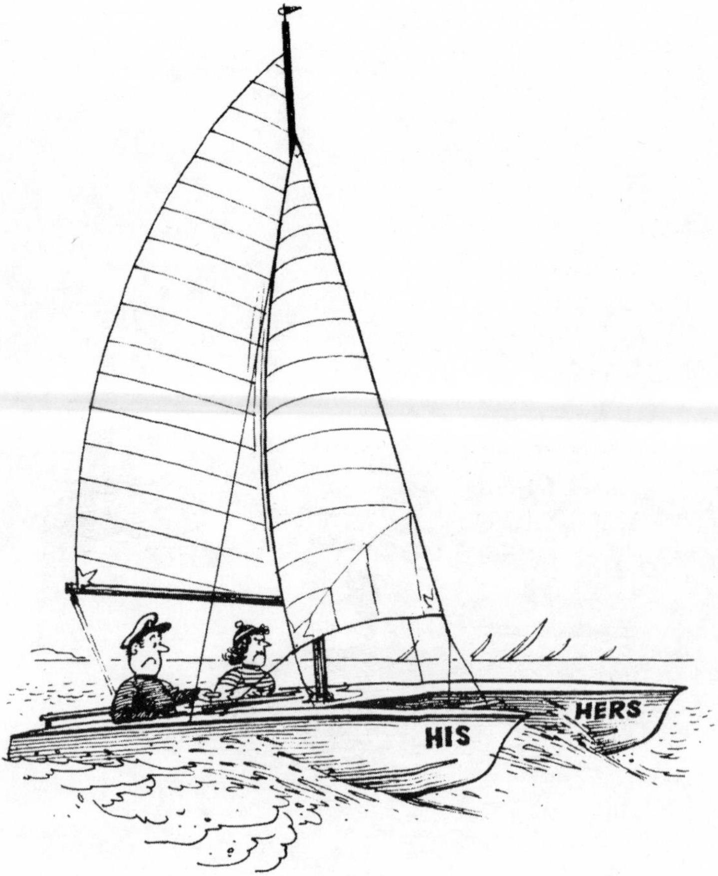
HIS
HERS

of being in sole command of your own boat.

'I'm NOT going to be rescued by Bob and
Vera Harrington.'

SAFETY FIRST

Make sure that your vessel is seaworthy before
setting sail.

Avoid weirs.

Do nothing that may alarm or annoy bathers.

Always step right into the centre of a small boat.

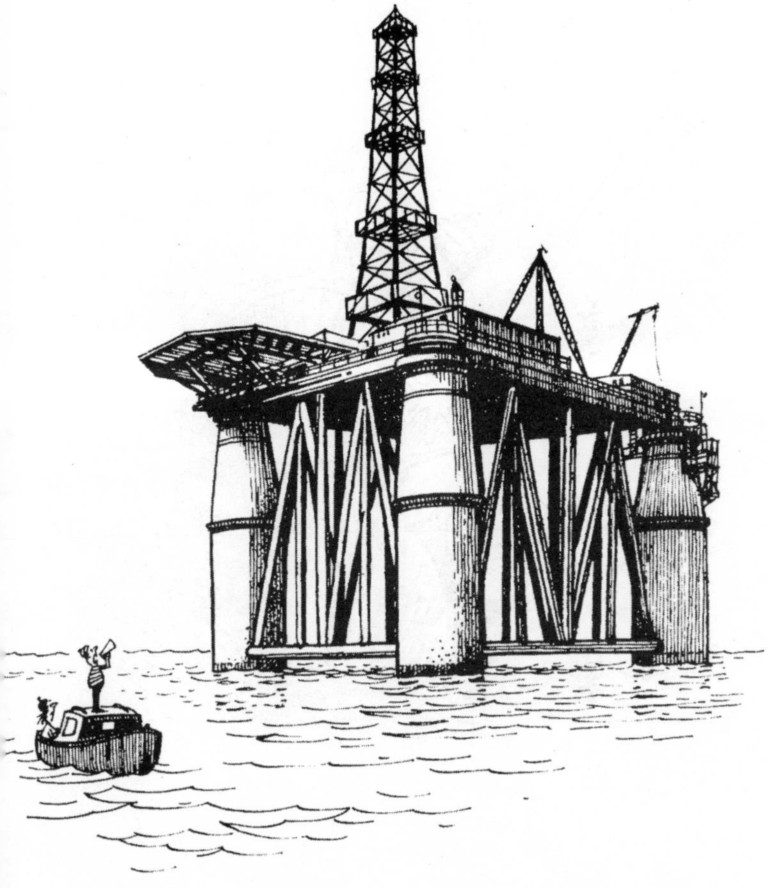

Always carry enough fuel – it is difficult to obtain at sea.

And never make any signals that may be mistaken for
a distress call.

Listen carefully to weather forecasts. And above all . . .

give your friends on shore precise details of where you
intend to sail

and make sure that each member of your crew is
wearing a life jacket.

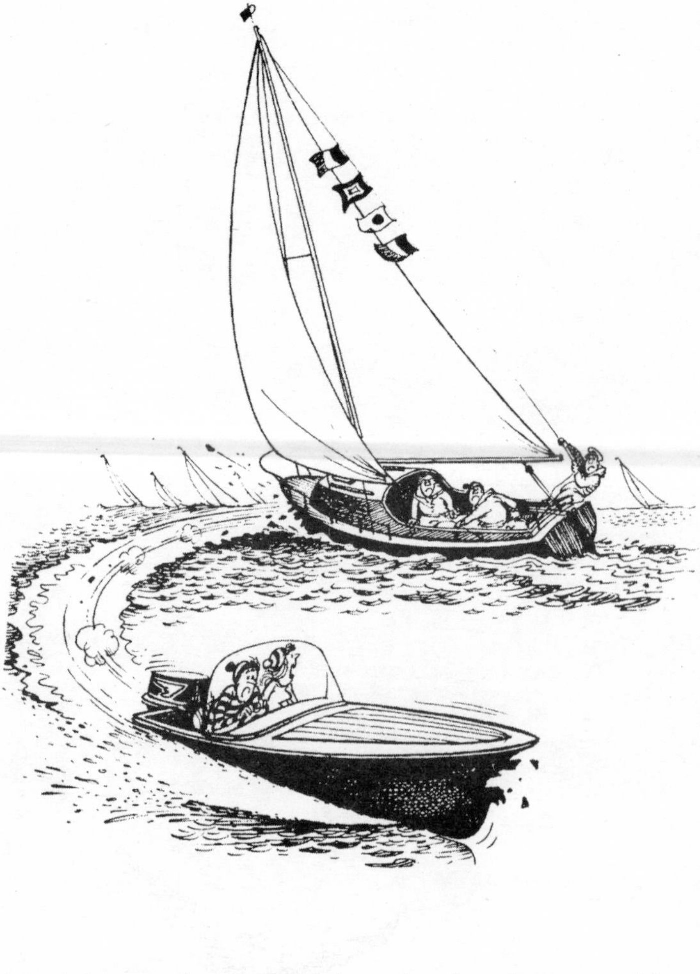

'I don't know what it means but it's a four-letter word.'

THE INTERNATIONAL
CODE OF SIGNALS

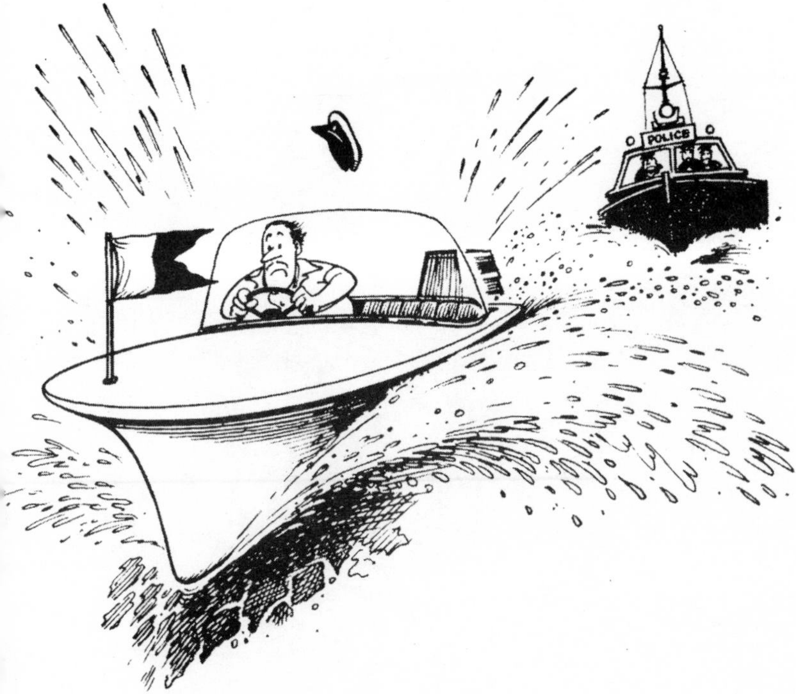
POLICE

I am undergoing a speed trial.

Man overboard.

I require a tug.

Stop your vessel.
I have something important to communicate.

I am manoeuvring with difficulty.

I am in need of a pilot.

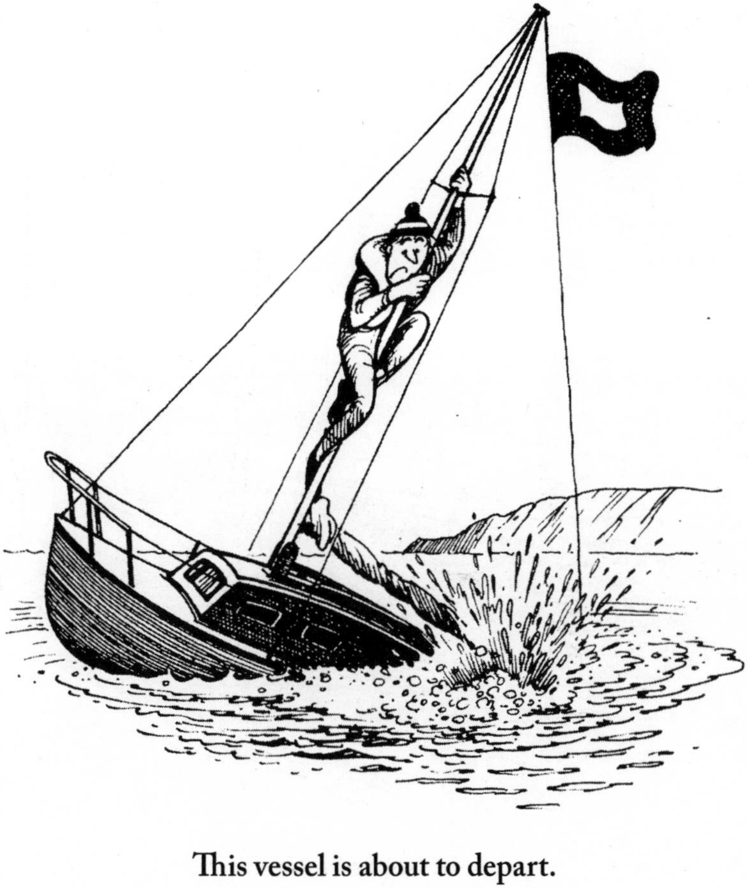

This vessel is about to depart.

Communicate with me.

Stop carrying out your intentions.

I have lost my bathing costume.

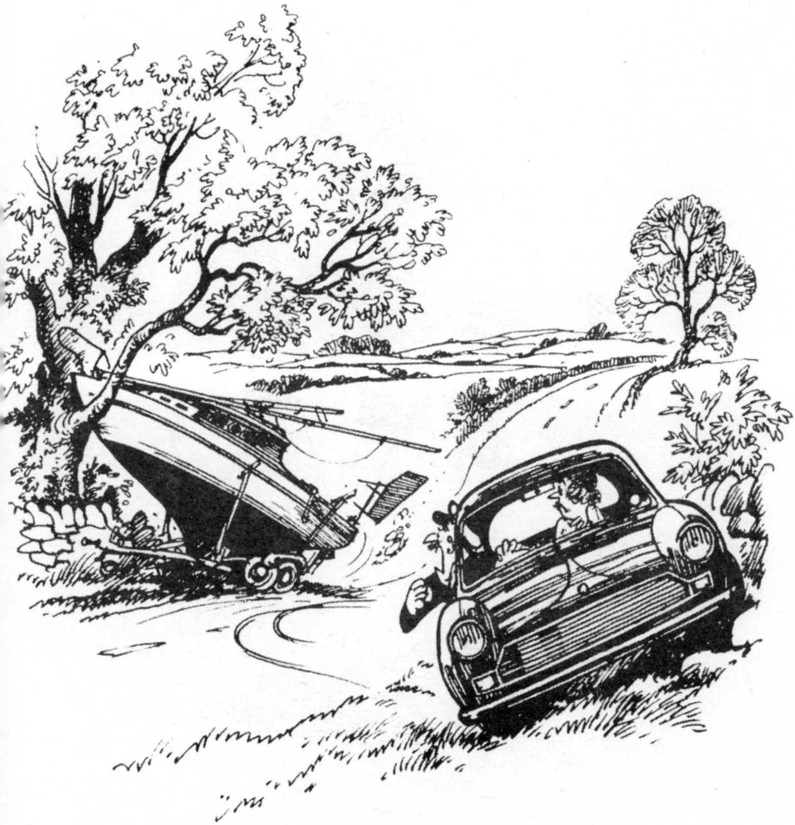

'A curse on that self-steering gear.'

RULES OF THE ROAD
FOR SAILORS

Clean off all barnacles – they will slow down
your progress.

Keep well clear of rocks when leaving harbour.

Organise the dog watch.

Check your craft for stowaways.

Beware of undertow.

Be prepared for sudden squalls

and if you run into fog – give one long blast.

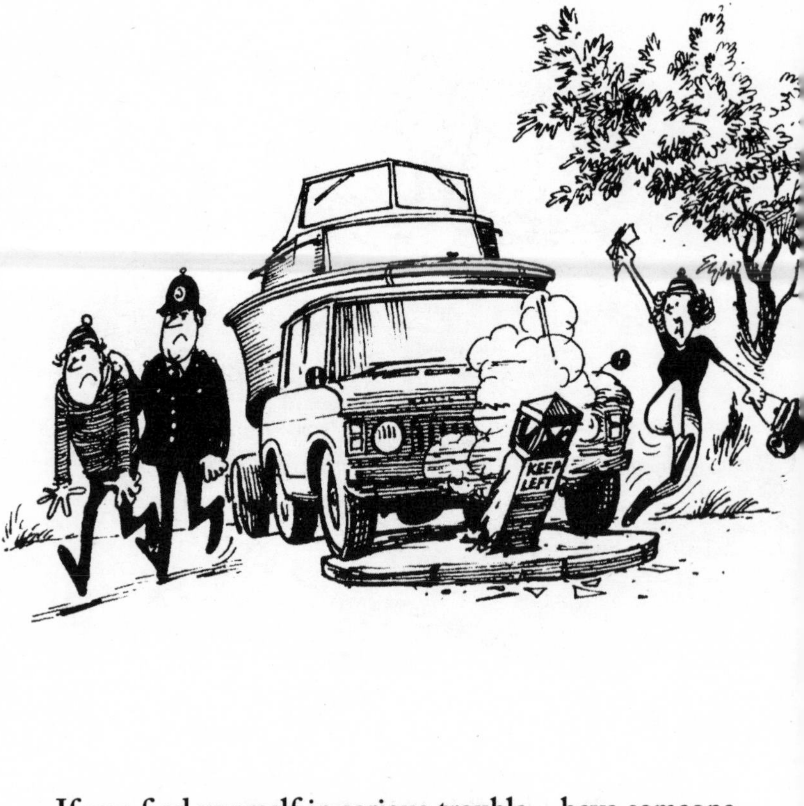
KEEP
LEFT

If you find yourself in serious trouble – have someone ready to bail you out.

Abandon ship only as a last resort.

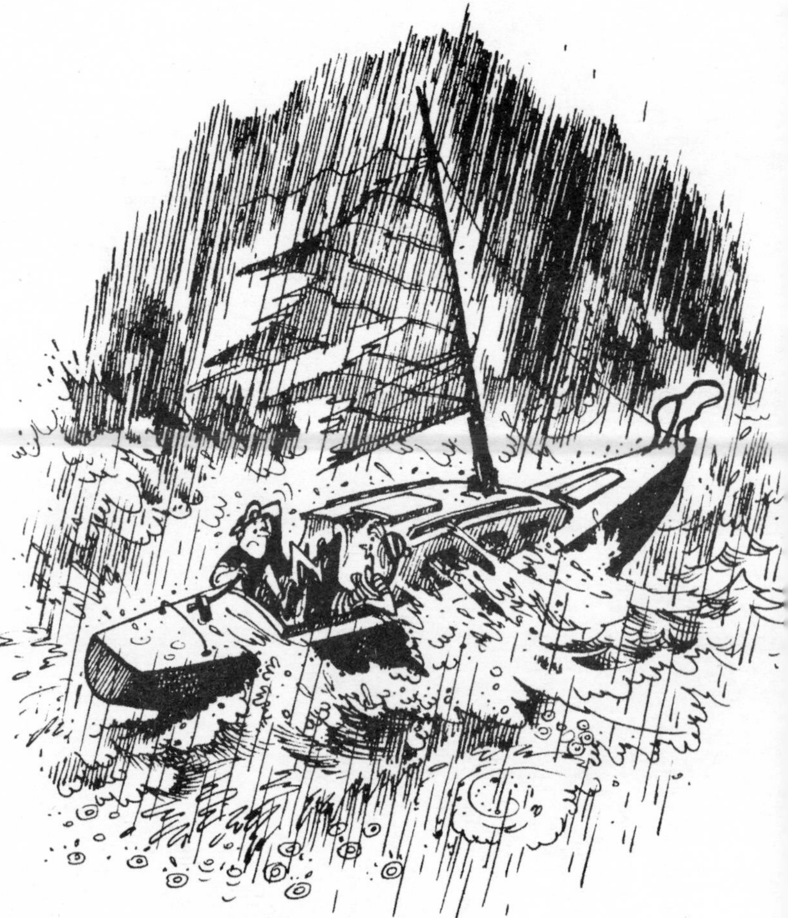

'If anyone hears the engine, we'll be ostracised at the club.'

GETTING THE WIND UP:
THE BEAUFORT SCALE

FORCE 0 Do not get impatient – you could be becalmed for weeks.

FORCE 1–2 You were warned to carry a spare
set of charts.

FORCE 3–4 You're glad she brought her mother
along now.

FORCE 5–6 ... And most of that's raw sewage.

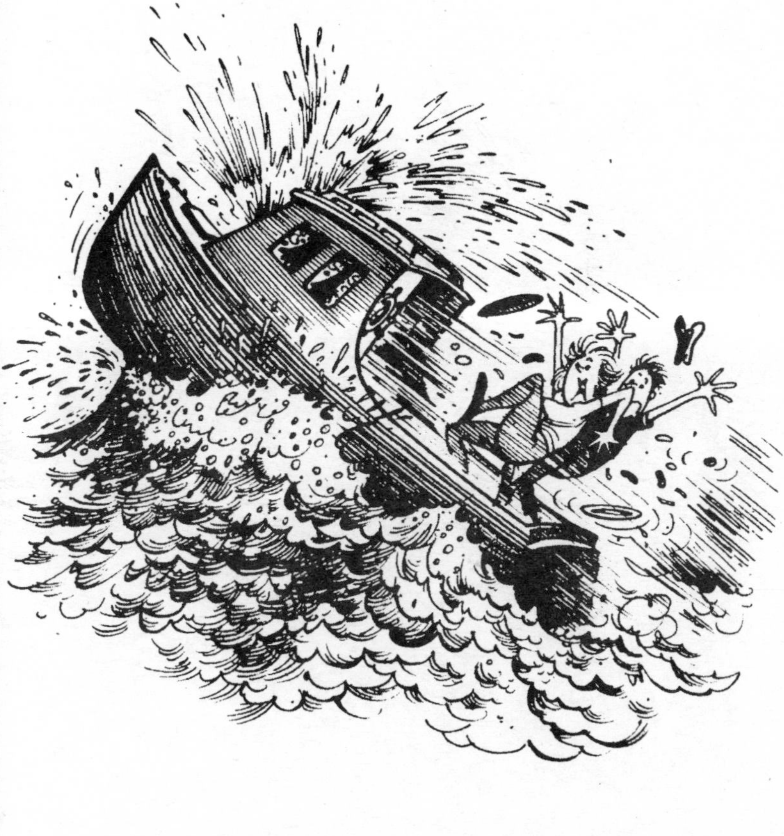

FORCE 7–8 Your dinner WAS in the oven.

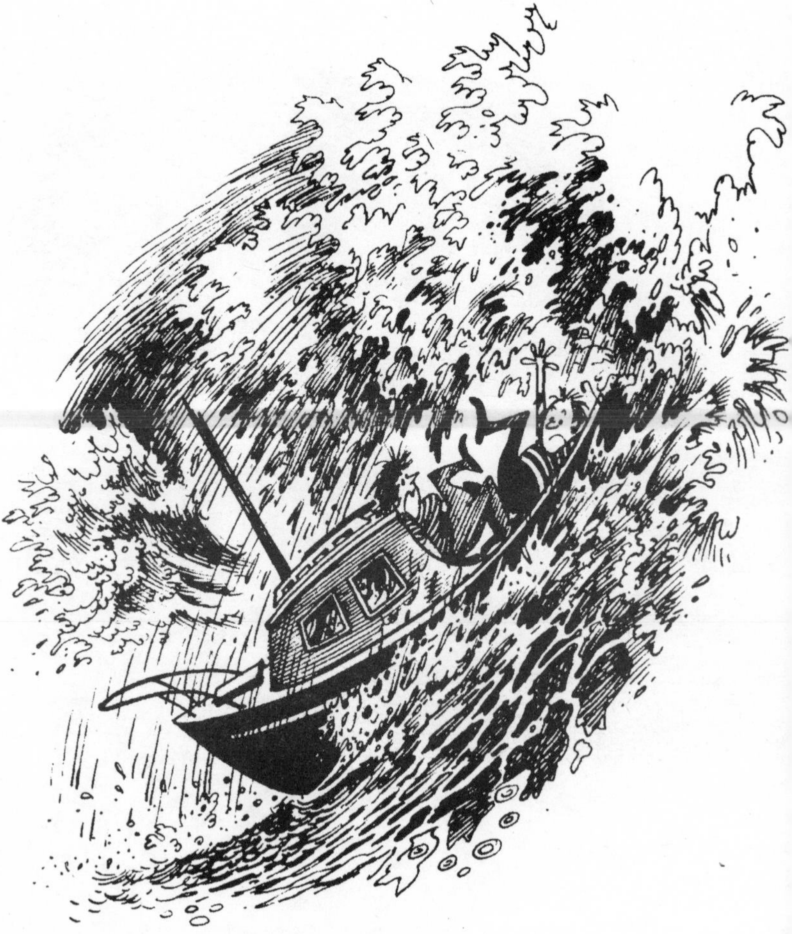

FORCE 9–10 It's going to be dicey getting her home up the A1.

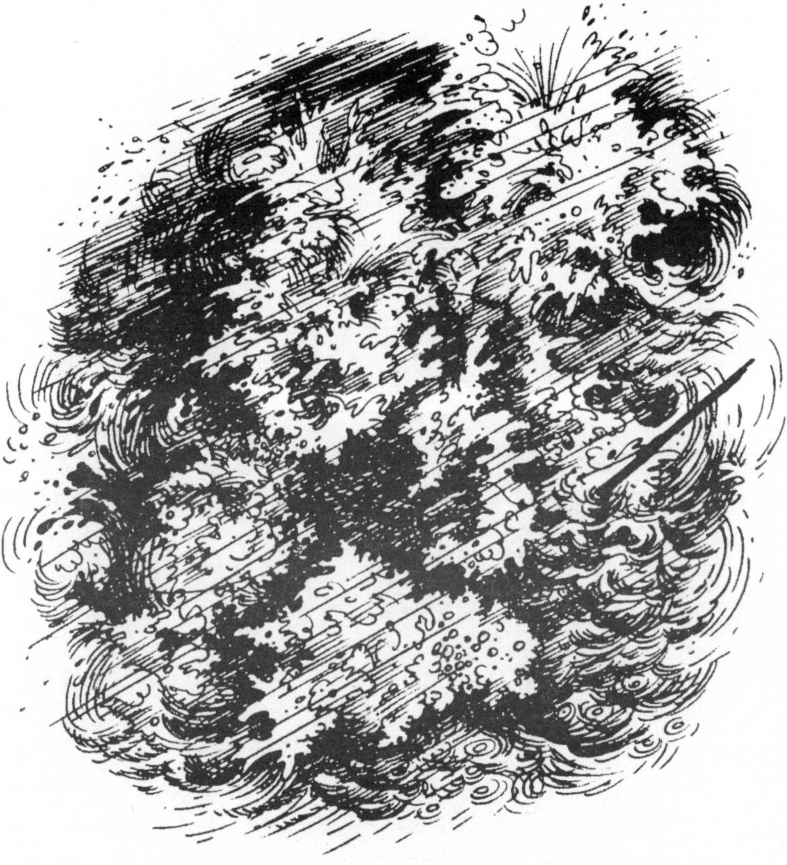

FORCE 11–12 Do not worry – your house blew down anyway.

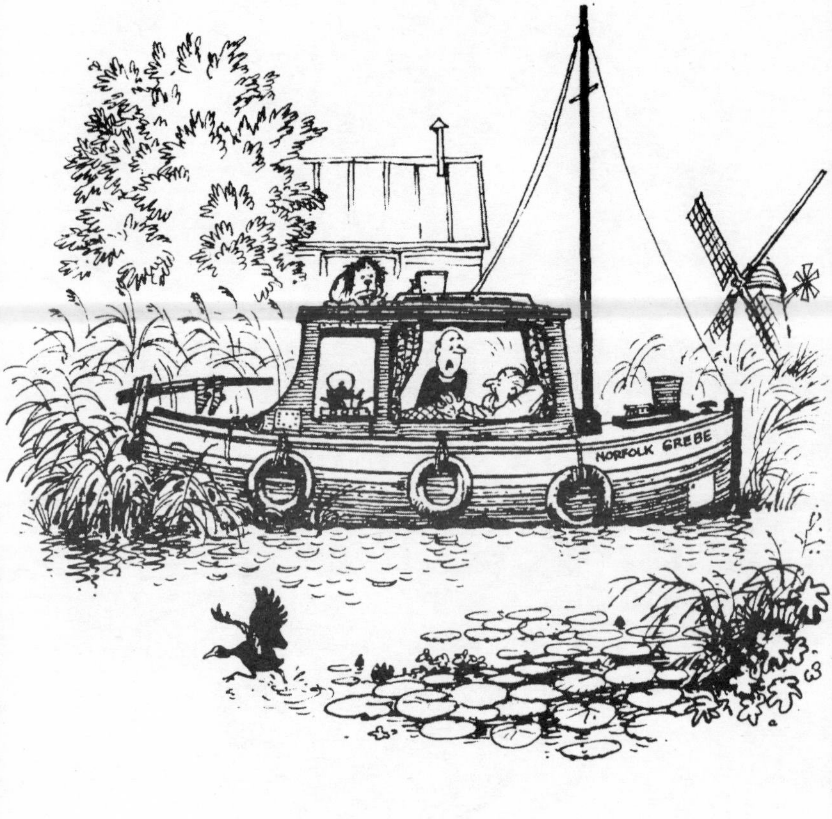
NORFOLK GREBE

'They'll allow me to bury you at sea but not in these waters, I'm afraid.'

SEA FEVER

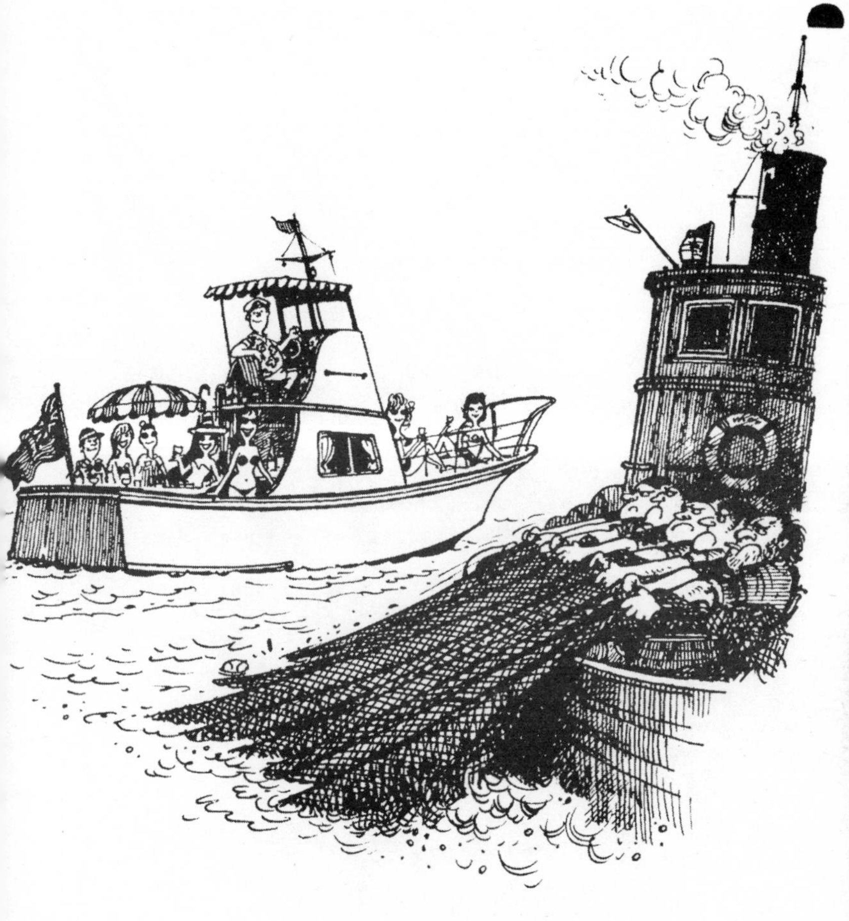

'Do you have any caviar?'

'I'm sorry mate but it's a single-handed race.'

'If you don't stop slimming, I'll have to look for fresh crew.'

'NOW can we start a family?'

'My God, Jackson! We're not going to make it.'

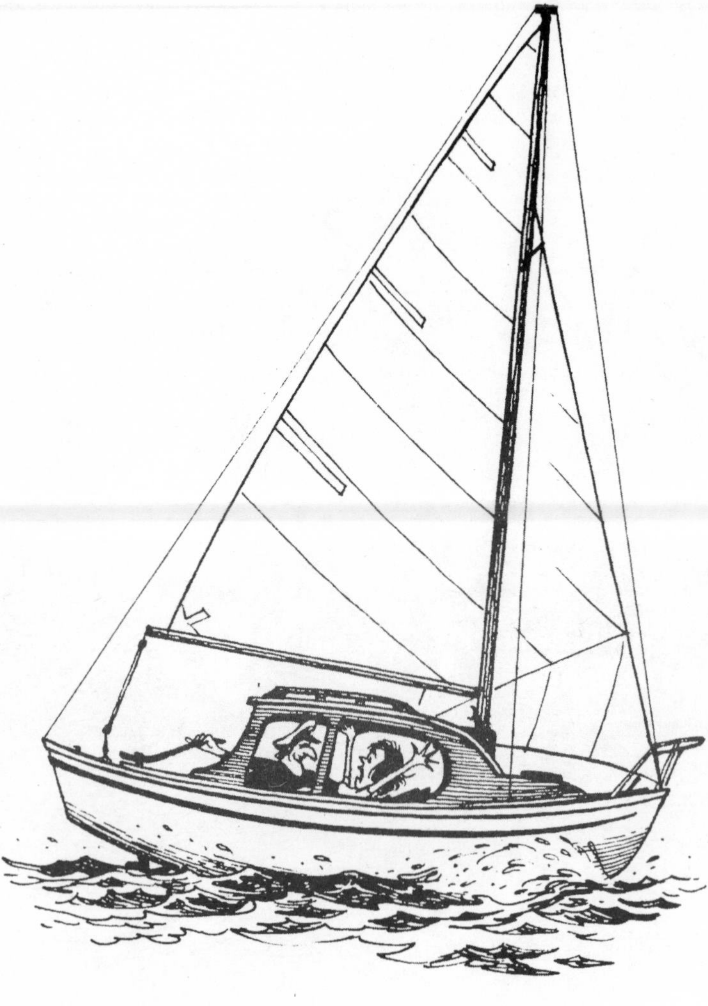

'You single-handed chaps are all the same.'

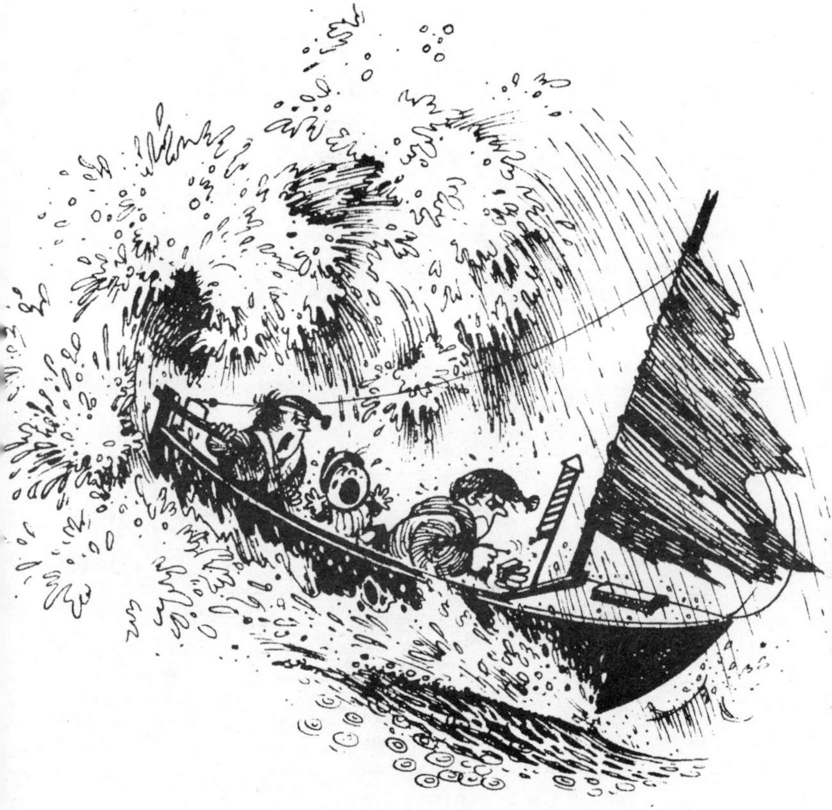

'Oh for pity's sake let him light it.'

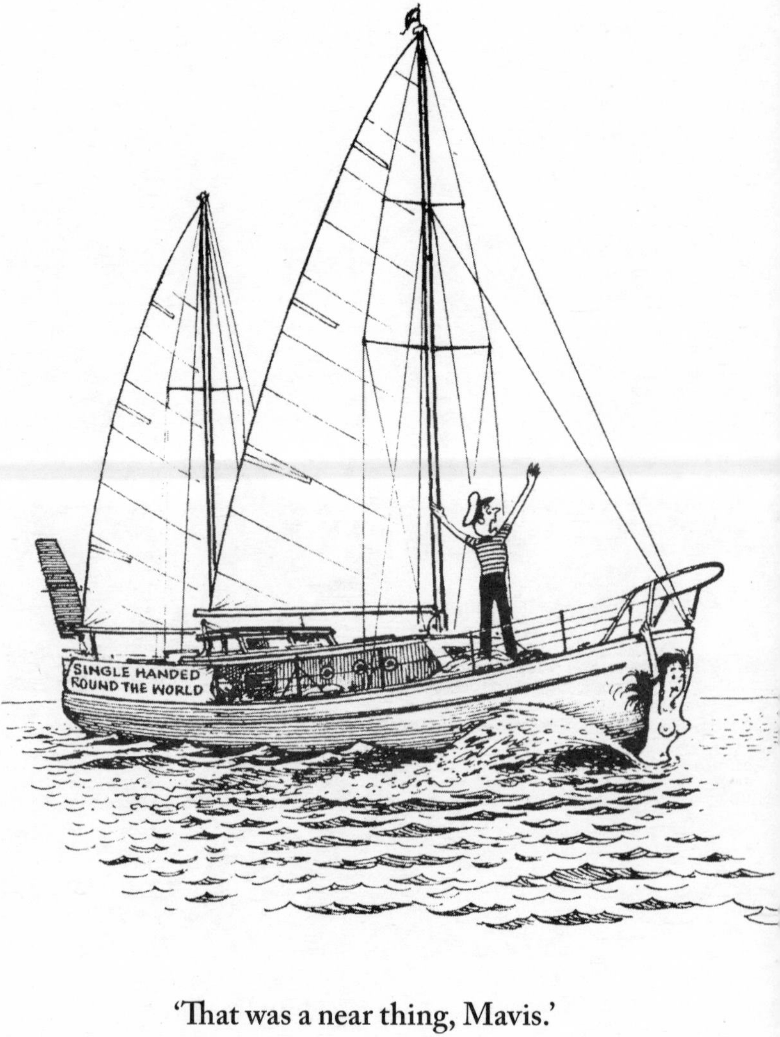
SINGLE HANDED
ROUND THE WORLD

'That was a near thing, Mavis.'

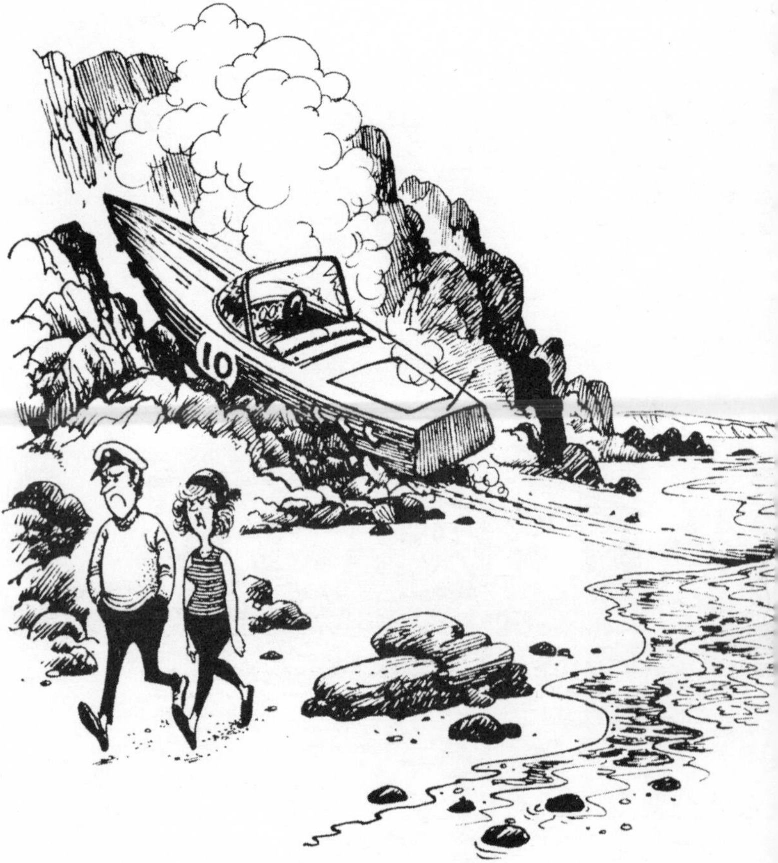
10

'I don't know why you race when you're
such a damn poor loser.'

'Remember that crump at the traffic lights?'

'What a stupid place to put an oil rig!'

'Navigation's easy – just follow the sewage back home.'

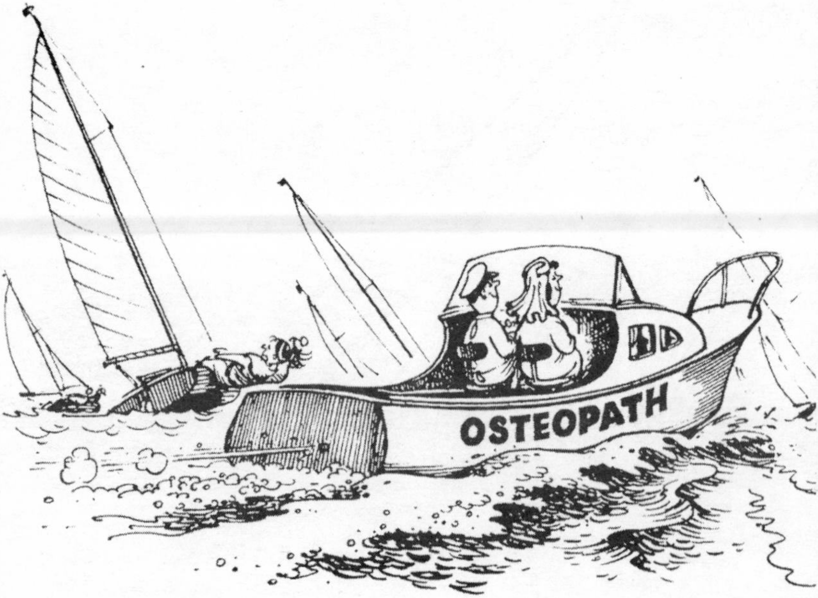
OSTEOPATH

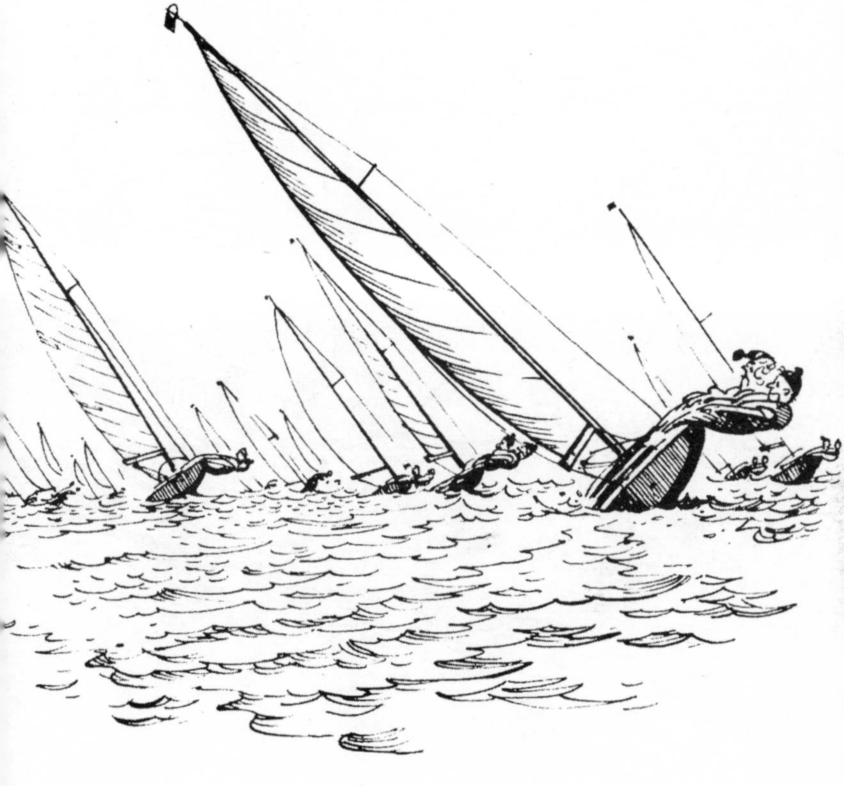

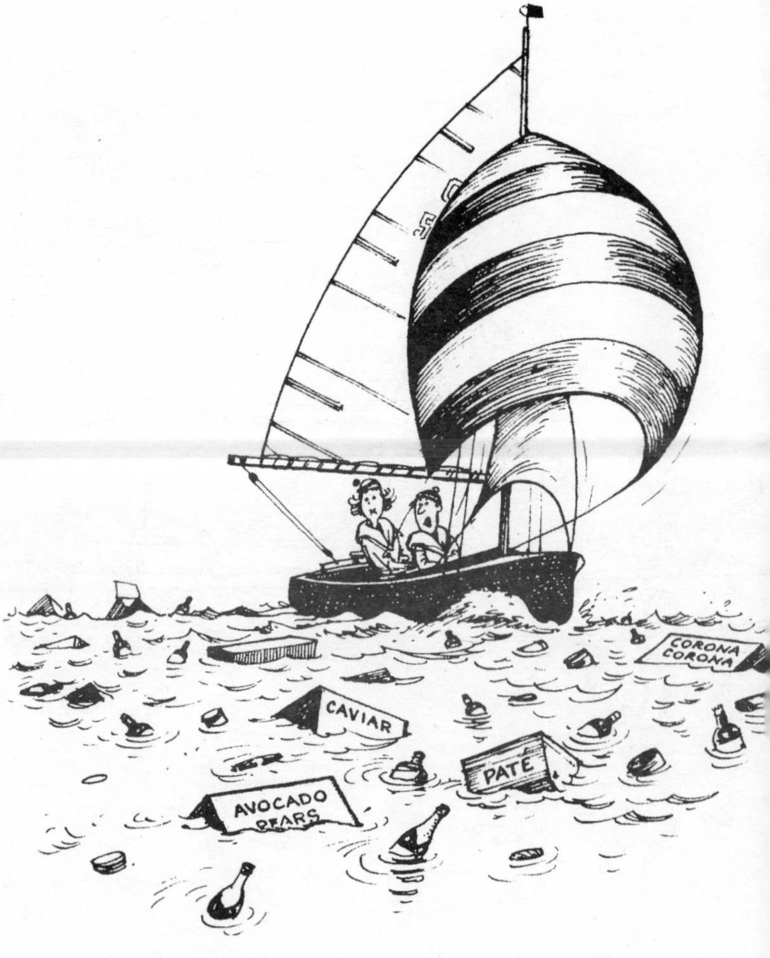
CORONA
CORONA
CAVIAR
PATÉ
AVOCADO
PEARS

'You can always tell when it's Cowes week.'

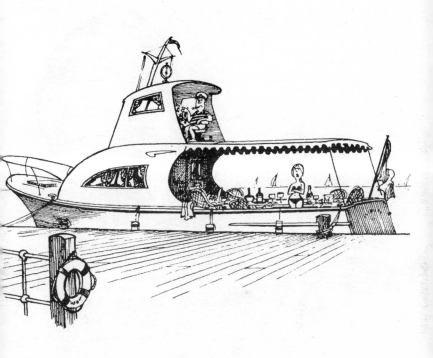

'The daily woman's late again!'

'Who's wearing stiletto heels?'

'Hello! The cargo's shifted.'

'He hates doing the weeding.'

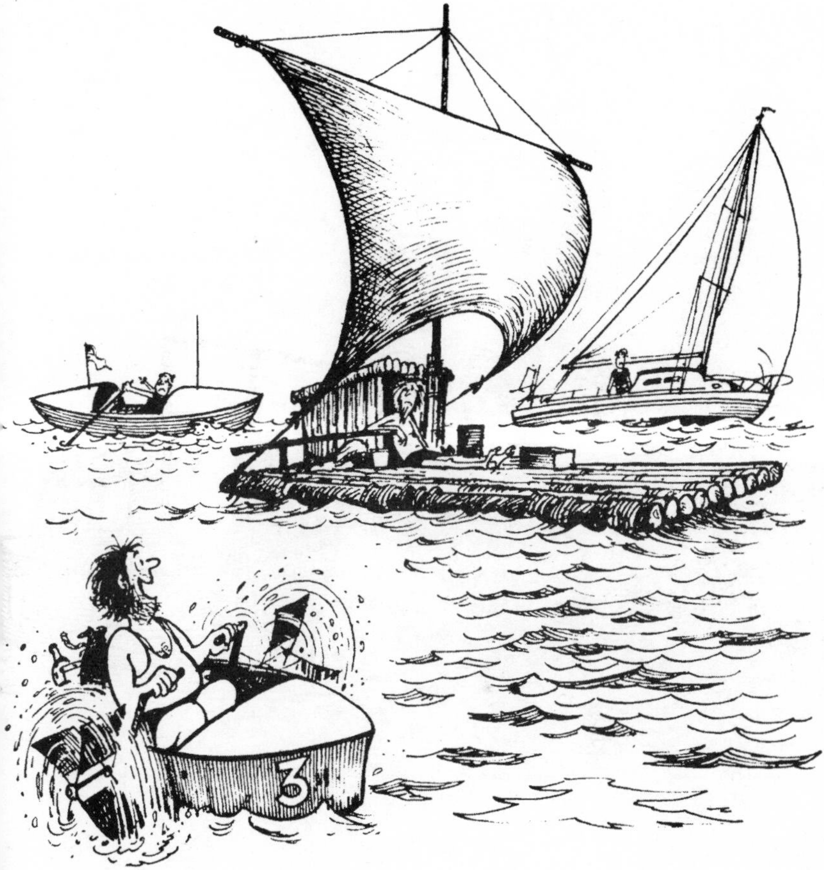
3

'They've been done! They've all been done.'

'Knee-deep in sawdust and shavings all winter – and
for what?'

ALSO IN THE SERIES

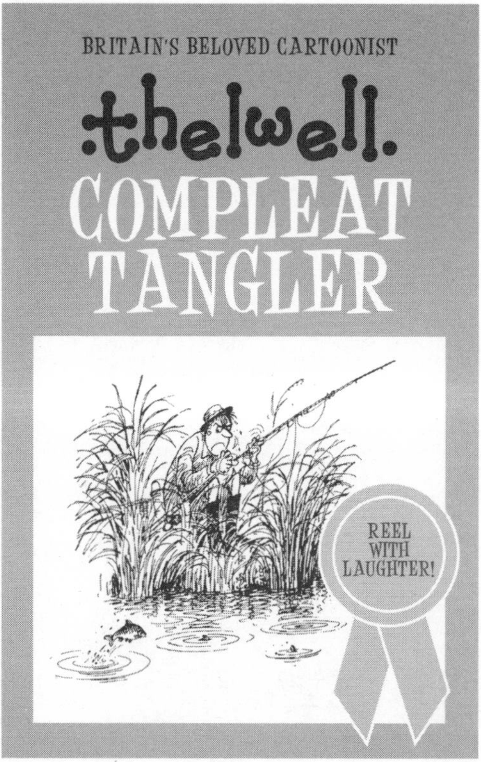
BRITAIN'S BELOVED CARTOONIST
thelwell.
COMPLEAT
TANGLER
REEL
WITH
LAUGHTER!

The perfect gift for any angler who appreciates the primitive thrill of hunting wild creatures, the hours spent studying minute aquatic flies, and the art of manipulating his tackle. Britain's beloved cartoonist Norman Thelwell creates reels of fun in his rip-roaring angler's guide.

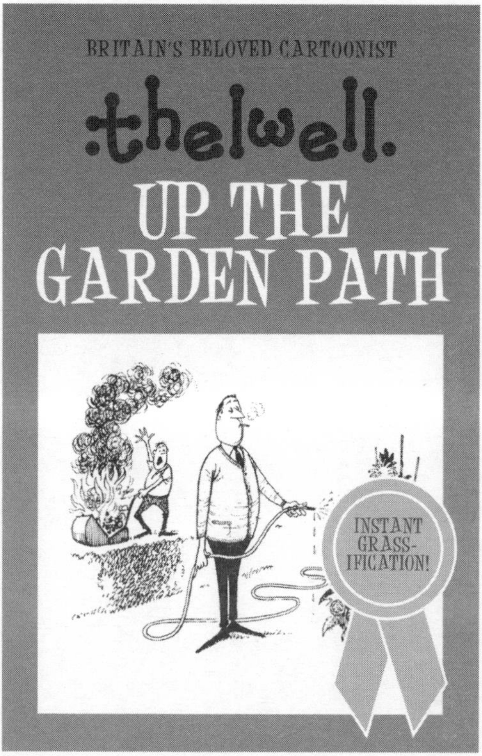
BRITAIN'S BELOVED CARTOONIST
thelwell.
UP THE GARDEN PATH
INSTANT GRASS-IFICATION!

The perfect gift for any gardener who has experienced overbearing neighbours, the pains of building a water feature, unruly indoor plants; and the battle to dig the lawnmower out from the shed. Britain's beloved cartoonist Norman Thelwell presents a fine crop of witticisms in his hilarious gardener's handbook.

The perfect gift for any golfer who has experienced the horrors of sporting the wrong attire on course, losing his ball, or been wronged by unforgivable gamesmanship. Britain's beloved cartoonist Norman Thelwell scores a hole-in-one with his rollicking golfer's manual.

To discover more great books and to
place an order visit our website at
www.allisonandbusby.com

Don't forget to sign up to our free newsletter at
www.allisonandbusby.com/newsletter
for latest releases, events and exclusive offers

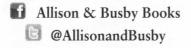 **Allison & Busby Books**
@AllisonandBusby

You can also call us on
020 7580 1080
for orders, queries
and reading recommendations